Pack
for a Picnic

Written by Anne Rooney
Photographed by Will Amlot

Collins

We see the sun.

It is good for a picnic.

I mix a good salad.

4

beetroot

carrots

peppers

mushrooms

radish

Emma packs further food.

chicken thigh

seeds

eggs

lentils

fish

Emma adds loads of pitta.

I pick a yogurt.

Emma fills cups under the tap.

I secure the hamper.

Now we march into the garden.

This dinner is good!

Picnic

 # After reading

Letters and Sounds: Phase 3

Word count: 60

Focus phonemes: /ee/ /oo/ /oo/ /igh/ /ur/ /er/ /ar/ /or/ /oa/ /ure/ /ow/ nn, rr, pp, gg, dd, tt

Common exception words: I, we, the, of, into

Curriculum links: Physical development: Health and self-care

Early learning goals: Reading: read and understand simple sentences, use phonic knowledge to decode regular words and read them aloud accurately, read some common irregular words

Developing fluency

- Your child may enjoy hearing you read the book.
- You could try taking turns to read a page. Model reading with lots of expression and encourage your child to do the same.

Phonic practice

- Practise reading multi-syllabic words together. Look at the word **picnic**. Ask your child to blend the letter sounds in each syllable chunk: pic/nic.
- Do the same with the following words:

  beetroot   beet/root

  peppers   pepp/ers

  mushrooms   mush/rooms

  lentils   len/tils

Extending vocabulary

- Look at page 4 together. Ask your child if they can think of another word that the author could have used instead of **good**. (e.g. *delicious, healthy*)
- Look at page 6 together. Ask your child if they can think of another word that the author could have used instead of **further**. (e.g. *more, extra*)
- Look at page 11 together. Ask your child if they can think of another word that the author could have used instead of **secure**. (e.g. *close, shut*)
- Look at page 12 together. Ask your child if they can think of another word that the author could have used instead of **march**. (e.g. *walk, go*)